The Adventures of Charlie Crab and Friends

Alan Williams & Amelia Williams

Published by Paul Smith Publishing London 2023

Copyright © Alan Williams & Caroline Hill 2023

Cover & Illustrations © Amelia Williams 2023

Edits Phil Williams & Caroline Hill

A CIP catalogue record for this title is available from the British Library

ISBN PB 978-1-912597-24-6
ISBN eBook 978-1-912597-25-3

Paul Smith Publishing
www.paulsmithpublishing.co.uk

For family...
Incredible life long memories, of holidays by the sea
Forever thankful

Bottom of the deep blue sea

Sammy Shrimp's Home
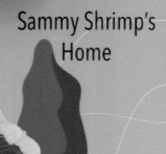

Horace the Hermit Crab's Home

The Rock Pools

Charlie Crab's Home

The Beach

And the first story begins…

Down at the bottom of the deepest pool
In the corner of the rock pools
All that could be seen were…
Two sharp pinchers and two black eyes.

Then out walked…Charlie Crab
Now, Charlie doesn't walk forwards
He doesn't walk backwards
He walks *sideways!*
Off he went along the bottom of the deep blue sea
to find his two friends
Horace the Hermit Crab and Sammy Shrimp.

As he rounded a small rock there was Sammy Shrimp

"Hello, Sammy," said Charlie Crab

"Hello, Charlie," replied Sammy Shrimp

"Have you seen Horace today, Sammy?" enquired Charlie

"No I haven't, unfortunately. And he has been far from happy lately."

That is odd. That doesn't sound like Horace at all, thought Charlie

"Come on, let's go and find him and cheer him up!"

The two friends started searching behind seaweed and around the bigger rocks, but there was no sign of Horace

They were about to give up, when they heard a long sigh followed by "Oh dear, dear, dear!"

Then there was another, deeper sigh, "No, it won't do!!"

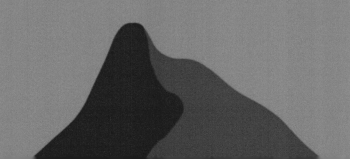

The two friends continued looking and listening
following the grumbling and the sighing
Finally, around the last big rock, Horace appeared
surrounded by a multitude of empty shells.

"What are you doing!?" exclaimed Charlie Crab

"Why all the moaning?" asked Sammy Shrimp

"You know I'm a hermit crab," said Horace

"I live in other creatures' empty shells

but I grow so quickly, they don't fit me any more

I have to find a new one." He gave a final long sigh.

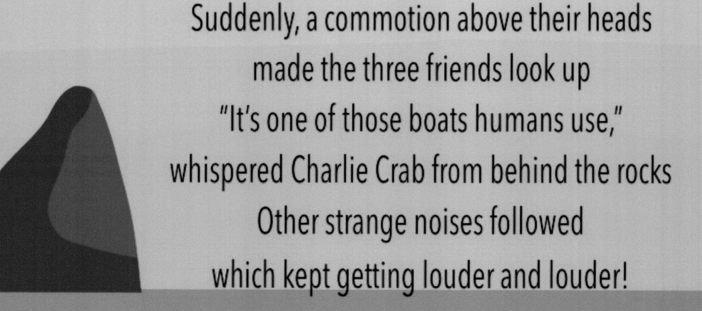

Suddenly, a commotion above their heads
made the three friends look up
"It's one of those boats humans use,"
whispered Charlie Crab from behind the rocks
Other strange noises followed
which kept getting louder and louder!

Plop! Ogle, Ogle, Ogle. Plop!!
Something landed almost on top of the three friends
nearly squashing them flat
"It's a bottle!!" hollered Charlie Crab
"More rubbish we don't want or need!" yelled Sammy Shrimp.

"Lovely!" said Horace the Hermit Crab excitedly

"LOVELY!?" shrieked Charlie Crab and Sammy Shrimp together

"Lovely," said Horace, "look, it fits me perfectly!"

"Hurray!!" cheered the three friends

"You will be the only Hermit Crab living in a bottle," declared Charlie Crab

"You are going to be famous!" shouted Sammy Shrimp

Horace the Hermit Crab smiled happily.

Suddenly, the sun sank down with a
PHSSSSSHH…
as it touched the sea.

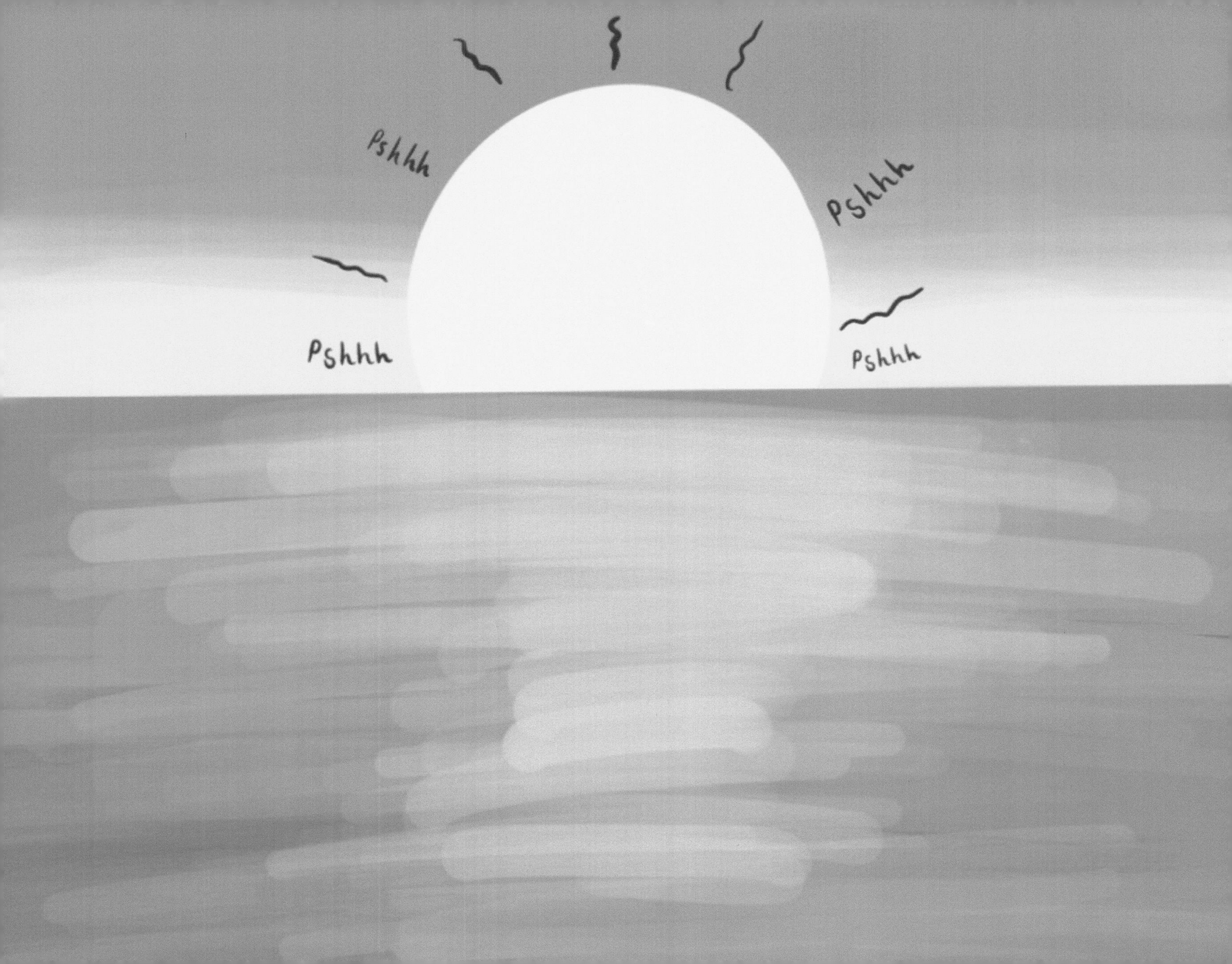
Pshhh
Pshhh
Pshhh
Pshhh

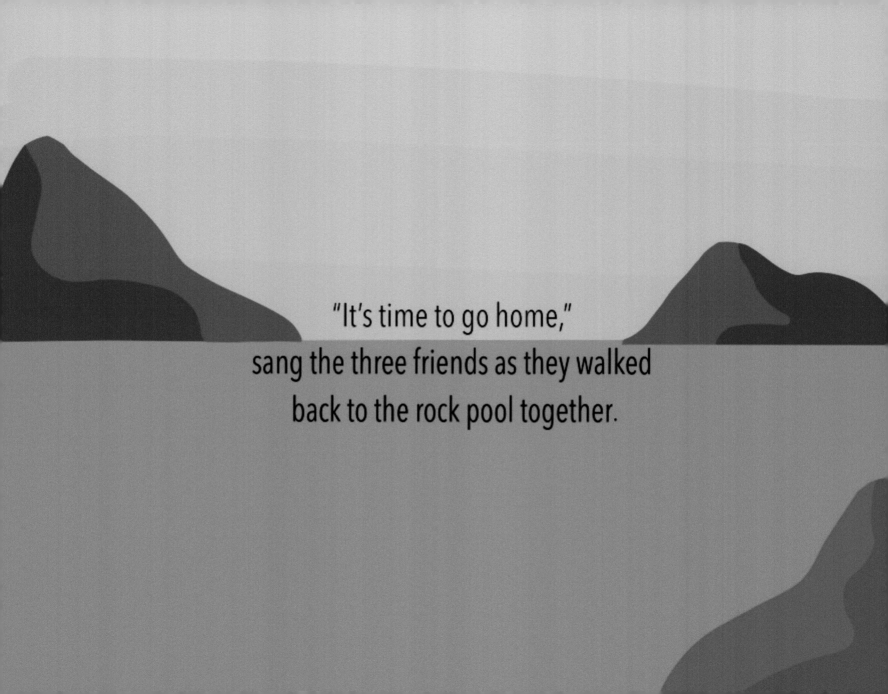

"It's time to go home,"
sang the three friends as they walked
back to the rock pool together.

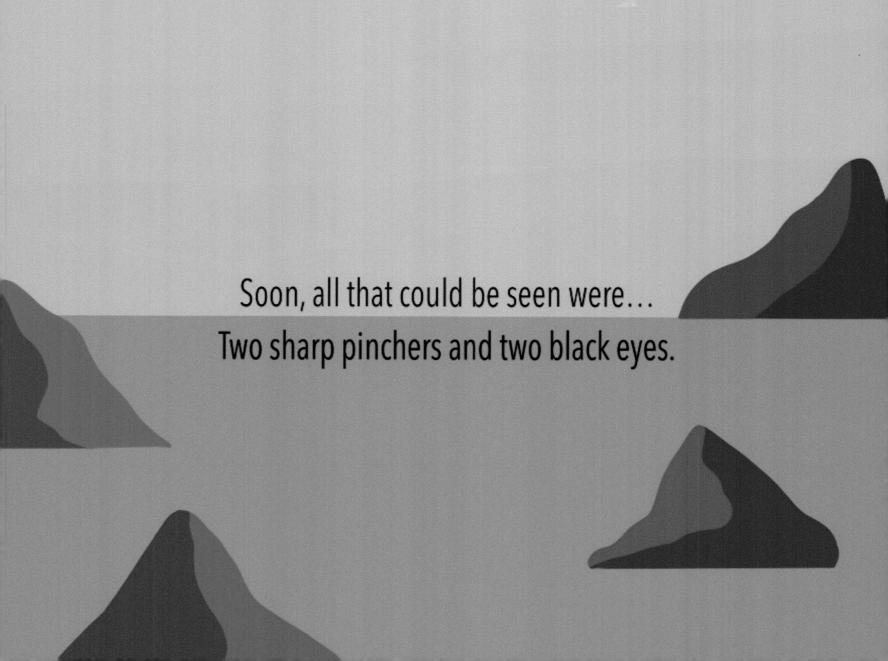

Soon, all that could be seen were...
Two sharp pinchers and two black eyes.

Recall and Comprehension Questions

- How many friends does Charlie Crab have

- Can you remember their names?

- In the story, Charlie asks Horace and Sammy questions; can you remember one of them?

- Why was Horace upset?

- What was the commotion above their heads?

- What made Horace happy again?

- What did the bottle nearly do to the three friends?

- What sound did the sun make as it touched the sea?

- Can you remember what the last thing that could be seen was?

New Vocabulary

In the story, there might have been words you weren't quite sure of. Here are four that I found:

1. Hollered
2. Commotion
3. Multitude
4. Enquired

• Do you know the meaning of the words above? If not, how could you find out?
• Can you find any other words you are not sure of?
• Can you make up a sentence that has one of these words in it?

Remember!

If you are writing or speaking your answers, they MUST make sense.
All sentences start with a capital letter and end in a full stop.
How did you get on with your answers?

Give yourself a score out of 5!